To My Parents

Words can never convey the profound gratitude and love
I have for you. I am so grateful to you for encouraging Mark
and me to experience so many exciting adventures together.

I am also very appreciative to you for giving us the confidence
and strength to get through difficult times and for all the sacrifices
you made to "open our eyes." Your love knew no bounds.

I learned at a young age what an amazing gift it is to grow up
in such a close, nurturing, and loving family.
I will love you...always.

150 East 52nd Street, Suite 32002
New York, NY 10022
www.lightswitchlearning.com

Educators and Librarians, for a variety of teaching resources, visit www.lightswitchlearning.com

Library of Congress Cataloging-in-Publication Data is available upon request.
Library of Congress Catalog Card Number pending

ISBN: 978-1-68265-353-1

The Boy Who Opened Our Eyes by Elaine Sussman
Illustrated by Anni Matsick

Book design by Kristine Bergenheim
The text of this book is set in Legacy Sans Book

Edited by Adam Reingold
Printed in China

2 3 4 5 6 7 8 9 10

The Boy Who Opened Our Eyes

by Elaine Sussman · illustrated by Anni Matsick

I know a six-year-old boy who is very, very special. He's my one and only brother, Mark. Most days, he makes us smile and laugh. Some days, he makes us feel sad. But every day, he opens our eyes with his amazing new surprises.

One day, when Mark was only two years old, Mom, Dad, and I were in the kitchen. And Mark... well, we thought he was napping on the living room sofa. Suddenly, we heard music.

Mark wasn't napping after all. He was alone and playing my toy piano. My tiny brother was tapping the keys with his delicate fingers. He was playing a song right in tune. We were stunned.

"Amazing! Look, he's playing Elaine's piano," Mom said with a big smile. "How could this be? He's never played any instrument before."

As we watched and listened, we saw how happy he was. From that moment on, Mark always filled our house and neighborhood with music.

Now, thanks to Mark, I also love music. He and I are alike in other ways, too, even though I'm four years older than he is. I'm ten years old, and he's six. We both love to get hugs and kisses from Mom and Dad. And we are both crazy about our fluffy little dog, Sparkie.

Sunday mornings are so exciting for Mark and me. We like to get up early, put on our chef's hats and aprons, and make scrambled eggs and pancakes for Mom and Dad. The aroma of the food smells so good. It makes us, and even Sparkie, so hungry. Sometimes, we end up eating everything ourselves before Mom and Dad even wake up.

We have fun doing so many things together. At night, we both giggle as we hide under my blanket and tell scary stories. After we fall asleep, we both also like to dream about the moon and stars and faraway places.

Mark and I are alike in some ways, but we are also different. He loves chocolate ice cream. I love vanilla. He likes to gallop on a horse. I like to trot. Mark plays in the big waves in the ocean, but I prefer to read a book safely on the beach.

Mark's a little daredevil. He does things that many kids are afraid to do. He climbs the tallest trees. He flies really high in the air on the swings at the playground. Mark has no fear of animals—not even of snakes or lizards. *They gross me out!*

Mark always seems to stay calm in scary situations. I don't. I'm a scaredy cat. He's really brave. I'm not. Once, when we were boating on a lake, our canoe tipped over. I was so scared. I grabbed onto the canoe and held on as tightly as I could. Not Mark! He just floated in the water, happy and smiling. He knew Dad would rescue us, and we would be okay.

It's important that Mark is brave and a bit of a daredevil. He has challenges that most other kids don't have.

My little brother Mark is blind. His eyes cannot see. Mark's world is dark.

10

Mark can't see anything, not even colors or shadows. He sees the world differently than we do, through touch, sound, taste, and smell. He is curious about many things. He tries to understand what sighted people can see.

Once, Mark asked, "Elaine, what's your favorite color?"

"Red," I replied.

"What does red *feel* like?" he asked.

"Red feels hot to the touch," I answered. "It's like touching a pot cooking on the stove."

He continued with his questions. "And what does red *taste* like?"

"Red tastes sweet, like apples, strawberries, and cherries," I said.

"What does red *sound* like?" Mark asked. He wanted to know more and more.

"Red is a color to get people's attention," I said. "Red is like a fire truck's siren."

"I think yellow is my favorite color," said Mark.

"Why yellow?" I asked.

"Mom told me that the sun is yellow," he said. "It feels warm on my skin. It makes me relax and feel comfortable. Yellow also tastes sweet like bananas."

"And what does yellow sound like?" I asked.

Mark thought. "It sounds like summer. It's full of kids who are laughing and playing and birds that are chirping."

It's challenging to be blind. Imagine trying to watch TV or cross the street without being able to see. The simplest things can be a challenge for Mark, but he often finds a way to succeed. It seems like every day he surprises us by doing something new.

One day not long ago, Mark decided to choose his clothes by himself without any help from Mom or Dad. He looked so proud and funny when we walked into the bedroom. He was wearing not only a big smile, but also a red sock on one foot and a white sock on the other. Even funnier than his choice of socks was the rest of his outfit. He had on my pink flowered pants, and he was wearing my yellow shirt backwards.

"Here I am!" he proudly exclaimed as he lifted his hands in the air and grinned.

We couldn't stop laughing at Mark's crazy outfit. That's when we started calling him "Mr. Mismatch."

All kids are unique. Many kids have special challenges. Some can't see...or hear...or walk...or learn the way other students do. For challenged kids, learning can be more difficult, but those challenges are just a part of who they are. Otherwise, they are just like typical children. All kids have their own skills and talents.

Mark loves music. He hears it on the radio and sings along all the time. He feels music everywhere. Sometimes, he beats his drum as he marches to the sounds of the vacuum cleaner. Other times, he taps his feet and sings along to the beat of the spinning washing machine.

Mark likes to sing and play all types of instruments, including the piano, drums, and ukulele. Music helps him express his feelings. He creates music and words that come from his heart. He sings his songs to family and friends of all ages. They are always happy when singing along with Mark and tapping their feet to his music.

Mark can feel left out when others are playing, but music comforts him. It takes away his feelings of loneliness. It also gives him confidence because he knows he can play by ear any song that he hears. This talent makes him feel welcomed by others.

Mom often says, "Music makes Mark feel and shine like the brightest star."

Mom is right. Mark does shine when he plays music. He's a star in other ways, too. At school, Mark struggled to learn how to read and write Braille. Blind people read Braille by gently touching tactile letters, which are raised dots on a page.

To help Mark learn to read, Mom spent many long hours learning Braille herself. She then practiced with Mark every day. Learning Braille was very difficult. It took a long time. But Mark is resilient—he kept at it. Finally, he learned to read whole books in Braille.

Learning to write Braille is another very difficult challenge. Mom spent months teaching Mark how to write using a Braille slate and stylus. With lots of determination, he was finally able to write all by himself.

Mark's world gets bigger with each book he reads. He loves reading to others and sharing stories. We were all so proud of Mark when he succeeded in learning Braille. Everyone is curious about Mark, the little boy who reads with his fingers.

Mark was so happy when people praised him for learning Braille. One kid, though, a boy named Walter, was jealous of Mark. He didn't want to see my brother get so much attention. He was so nasty that he taunted and teased Mark all the time.

One day, Mark woke up feeling horrible. He was shaking. He was scared and didn't want to go to school. Mark knew that the bully, Walter, was going to pick on him again.

After breakfast, my brother and I walked to the bus stop. Many of the kids in the neighborhood waited together, including Walter, the big, mean bully. Soon, our bus arrived to take us to school.

In the bus, Walter suddenly hollered at Mark, "Hey, you! Shorty!"

Walter then grabbed Mark's favorite baseball cap off his head.

"Look at this," he yelled to the other kids, waving my brother's cap.

"Please give me my hat," Mark said fearfully.

The bully then threw Mark's hat to the back of the bus. A girl picked up my brother's hat and gave it back to him. Mark was grateful to her for being so kind. Still, he remained scared because he didn't know what to do about the bully. He just wanted to crawl under the seat and hide.

Mark usually ate lunch with his friend Steve, but today, his pal was absent. In the lunchroom, Mark heard kids talking at a table, so he reached for an empty chair and started to sit down.

"You can't sit here," Walter threatened. "This table is saved for my friends only."

Again, Mark was upset and frightened by Walter's taunting. So my brother quickly searched for the nearest table and ate all by himself. He felt so alone that he just wanted to disappear.

Being bullied frightened Mark. It upset Mom, Dad, and me, too. We couldn't sleep that night because we were so worried about Mark. The next day, I told some of our friends that Mark felt nervous and scared. They understood. They refused to let Mark be bullied anymore. They told Walter that he wasn't being nice.

Carlos was really mad. "Stop being so mean," he yelled at Walter.

Ron was mad, too. "Just because he's small and can't see doesn't make it okay for you to pick on him!" Ron screamed.

Kim joined in. "Be kind to others. It will make you feel good."

Ivy gently put her arm around Mark to calm him and said, "It's always best to walk away from a bully."

"Thanks for being my friends and sticking up for me," Mark then said to Carlos, Ron, Kim, and Ivy. "I feel better now that you all protected me. I was really scared."

So Mark and his friends walked away. Walter was left all alone, without any friends.

Later that day, I called Ivy to thank her for sticking up for Mark. As Mom says, Ivy has lots of empathy—she's sensitive to other people's feelings. That's why she's my best friend!

"How's Mark doing?" Ivy asked. "Is he okay?"

"He's better," I answered. "He's much calmer, thanks to you and our friends who stood up for him."

"I know it's sometimes hard having a brother who has special needs," Ivy said. "You are an amazing sister to Mark. And he's an amazing brother to you, too."

"Thanks, Ivy," I replied. "I didn't know what to do when Mark was being bullied. I just wish some people were nicer and could understand and respect others."

"I know," Ivy said. "People should show more tolerance for others who are different from them. Because of Mark, I've learned that everyone is different and everyone has difficult challenges."

"Yes, you're right, Ivy," I added. "It's been a hard day. Thanks to you and our friends, I think Walter has learned his lesson and will leave Mark alone. See you tomorrow."

Sometimes, Mark struggles, but he tries to learn something new every day. He always asks questions because he's so curious. He makes us smarter because we have to create new ways to explain things to him. Then he can visualize and understand what we are describing.

One night, as we were heading to bed, Mark asked, "Elaine, can you tell me what clouds look like?"

"Hmm," I thought to myself. "How can I explain that?"

Suddenly, I figured it out. I ran and got a handful of cotton balls, and I had Mark touch them.

"Wow!" Mark said. "I didn't know clouds were so light and fluffy."

"You're right," I answered. "That's why they can float so high in the sky."

He continued to bombard me with questions. "What do the sun, moon, and stars look like?"

I had to think hard. That was a tough question!

I then picked up a small lamp and very carefully moved it close to his face. "This is hot and bright, like the sun," I said.

After that I moved the lamp farther away. He could barely feel its heat. "That's the moon," I explained.

"What about the stars?" he asked.

I wasn't sure what to say or do.

Suddenly, I had an idea. I took the lamp and again gently placed it near his face. This time I wiggled my fingers in front of the lamp.

"I feel the light moving. Are those twinkling stars?" he asked excitedly.

"Yes," I replied, "That's what stars look like."

Dad is also always dreaming up new ways to explain things that Mark can't see or understand. One day, Dad called to Mark and said, "It's windy today, so it's a perfect day to fly a kite in the park."

"What's a kite?" Mark asked.

Dad then showed one to Mark.

"This is how it feels," he said, letting Mark gently run his hands over the kite.

Dad continued, "And this is the tail." Now Mark's sensitive fingers touched the long tail.

"How high does it fly?" Mark asked.

"It flies so high that sometimes I can hardly see it," Dad answered.

Dad then carefully tied bells to the tail of the kite. As it started to fly up in the air, the bells rang loudly and clearly. As it soared higher and higher, Mark felt the tension in the kite string increase, and the bells were harder to hear.

"The kite is so quiet," Mark said.

"Yes," Dad replied. "It's soaring high, high up in the sky."

Thanks to Mark, many days are full of new adventures and excitement for all of us. Some days, though, are filled with sadness and difficulty, like the time when Mark was bullied. But every day, my little brother is kind and caring towards others. Every day, he inspires us to learn many new things.

Although Mark is blind, that doesn't mean he can't see. He just sees things in a different way, a very special way. If Mark is your friend, he's your friend forever. He'll hug you and know who you are by gently touching your hair. He'll never forget you.

"It's nice to see you!" he'll say with a warm smile.

My brother is like no one else. He'll show you the bright side of life. If you are his friend, he will open your eyes forever.

Elaine's Dream Comes True

It all started with a fifth grade homework assignment. The first week of school, our teacher told us to spend the weekend writing about anything that we felt was important or interesting to us. I knew exactly what I would write about. So I went home and began composing a poem about my brother, Mark.

When we returned to school on Monday, we all had to read our assignments in front of the class. As I began reading my poem, the kids grew silent. The teacher and the students were fascinated to hear about my little brother, who could not see.

At that moment, I knew what I wanted to do one day—write a story about Mark. My poem inspired me to write this book and fulfill my lifelong wish.

I hope that each one of you will always remember to try very hard to do as I did...
Follow your dreams and never give up.

I Know a Little Boy

I know a little boy
Who is everyone's joy.
He's only six years old,
But it must be told
He loves all the girls,
Especially ones with long curls.

A happy little boy is he,
Although his eyes cannot see.
With his hands and ears so keen,
His blindness hardly can be seen.

Bicycles and roller skates and ball,
Swimming and wrestling ... and sometimes a fall,
These and many other things he does so well,
Along with math and reading, he loves to spell.

A happy little boy is he,
Although his eyes cannot see.
His musical talents bring him joy every day,
And his challenges he faces in a positive way.

A wonderful little boy is he,
And if I'm prejudiced—please forgive me.
You see, this little boy Mark is no other
Than my one and only beloved brother.

You must be wondering…what became of Mark? Well, his love of music grew stronger and stronger. After much practice and determination, he became a professional singer, songwriter, and guitarist. He performed around the country.

Mark's greatest achievement was when he composed the music and lyrics to his patriotic song called "Our Prayers Go With You." He wrote this song for the Apollo 11 astronauts, who landed on the moon for the first time ever. Mark performed his song on various TV channels as the moon landing was about to take place. After the astronauts' historic mission, Mark was invited to perform his song at a special banquet in their honor.

Mark is still an avid reader and animal lover. He also enjoys traveling, exercising, playing the guitar and clarinet, and learning different languages.

Mark continues to sing and perform in community productions and at children's facilities and senior centers. As always, music remains close to Mark's heart.

Mark recently entertaining in Boca Raton, Florida.

Mark performing the song "New York, New York."

Depth of Knowledge

Discussion Questions

1 How are Mark and Elaine alike? How are they different?

2 In what ways are you like your brother, sister, or friend? How are you different?

3 What challenges do blind people face? What conclusions can you make about these challenges?

4 Have you faced challenges in life? Describe how you overcame your challenges.

5 Think of a product that would help a blind person do a simple everyday task. What would this product be? How would it work?

6 What conclusions can you make about pages 10–11? Why are these pages dark?

7 Read the following sentence from page 17: "Music makes Mark feel and shine like the brightest star." What does the author mean when using the words "brightest star"?

8 According to the author, how did Mark open people's eyes to see new things?

9 What is a bully? Describe the different ways that people can be bullied.

10 Read pages 28–29. Why did Dad put bells on Mark's kite? How would you help Mark sense something that is far away?

See page 38 for unique Braille activities.

Activities

1. Do you know someone like Mark who has overcome special challenges? Write a story about him or her and share it with the class.

2. Review the glossary on page 36. Select three glossary words and draw a picture describing each word. Include a definition in your own words below each drawing.

3. Read pages 24–25 to understand how Elaine thanks Ivy for showing empathy towards Mark. Write a letter to a friend thanking him or her for showing empathy towards you. Include examples of his or her actions showing that your friend cared about you.

4. Design a poster that highlights five rules about preventing bullying in your school.

5. Write a song describing how people are alike and different, and why it is important to respect people's differences.

Group Activity

Understand and prevent bullying
Write anti-bullying sayings on colored posters.

Discuss in groups
- Reflect on a time when you were bullied or when you were a bystander. Explain how you will change your actions in the future.

- Write your own anti-bully statements on your colored poster. Include one saying from the story, such as: "Be kind to others. It will make you feel good."

- After completing your statements, share them with the class.

- Display the anti-bullying statements on a hallway bulletin board.

Glossary

Aroma *(noun)* (ah **ROH** mah) a pleasant smell *(p. 6)*

Bombard *(verb)* (bahm **BAHRD**) to bother without any letup *(p. 26)*

Braille *(noun)* (**BRAIL**) a system of writing for blind people using letters that are raised dots *(p. 18)*

Bully *(noun)* (**BU** lee) someone who frightens, hurts, or threatens other people *(p. 20)*

Challenge *(noun)* (**CHAL** enj) something that is hard to do *(p. 9)*

Confidence *(noun)* (**KAHN** fih dents) a feeling that you can do something well *(p. 17)*

Daredevil *(noun)* (**DAIR** dev ihl) a person who does dangerous things *(p. 8)*

Delicate *(adjective)* (**DEL** ih kiht) very sensitive *(p. 4)*

Empathy *(noun)* (**EM** puh thee) the ability to understand and relate to another person's feelings *(p. 24)*

Express *(verb)* (ihks **PRES**) to talk or write about things you are feeling *(p. 17)*

Gallop *(verb)* (**GA** lep) the way a horse moves when it is running fast *(p. 8)*

Grateful *(adjective)* (**GRAYT** ful) feeling or showing thanks *(p. 21)*

Inspire *(verb)* (ihn **SPI** uhr) to cause someone to have a feeling or emotion *(p. 30)*

Mismatch *(noun)* (mihs **MACH**) two or more things that do not go together well *(p. 15)*

Outfit *(noun)* (**OUT** fiht) set of clothes worn together *(p. 15)*

Praise *(verb)* (**PRAYZ**) to say or write good things about someone or something *(p. 20)*

Resilient *(adjective)* (rih **ZIHL** yent) able to recover quickly after something bad happens *(p. 18)*

Slate *(noun)* (**SLAYT**) a frame used to hold paper and serve as a guide when writing Braille *(p. 18)*

Soar *(verb)* (**SOR**) to fly high in the sky *(p. 29)*

Special Needs *(noun)* (**SPE** shel **NEEDZ**) educational requirements of students who have learning challenges *(p. 24)*

Stun *(verb)* (**STUHN**) to surprise very much *(p. 4)*

Stylus *(noun)* (**STI** les) a tool with a hard point used to make raised dots to write Braille *(p. 18)*

Tactile *(adjective)* (**TAK** til) relating to the sense of touch *(p. 18)*

Talent *(noun)* (**TA** lent) a special ability that allows someone to do something well *(p. 17)*

Taunt *(verb)* (**TAWNT**) to say mean things to a person in order to make the person angry or sad *(p. 20)*

Tease *(verb)* (**TEEZ**) to bother a person in a way that is unfriendly and unkind *(p. 20)*

Tension *(noun)* (**TEN** shen) a condition of being stretched tight *(p. 29)*

Threaten *(verb)* (**THRE** ten) to say something that suggests you are going to hurt another person *(p. 21)*

Tolerance *(noun)* (**TAH** le rents) the willingness of a person to accept people who are different from him or her *(p. 25)*

Trot *(verb)* (**TRAHT**) the way a horse moves at a speed faster than walking *(p. 8)*

Ukulele *(noun)* (yoo ke **LAY** lee) a small guitar with four strings *(p. 17)*

Unique *(adjective)* (yoo **NEEK**) very special or unusual *(p. 17)*

Visualize *(verb)* (**VIH** shoo liz) to form a picture in your mind about someone or something *(p. 26)*

Acknowledgments

My special thanks to you, Mark: Because of you, this book came to be. You are my hero. You bring a ray of sunshine into the lives of all who know you. You really are something special. You opened my eyes forever.

To my one-of-a-kind husband, Joe: Thank you from the bottom of my heart for your unconditional love, support, patience, and humor. Without your willingness to help around the house, I could never have toiled for endless hours on this project. Most of all, I thank you for always being so loving towards Mark and bringing so much joy into his life every day.

To my sons, Steve and Ronnie: You are both—without a doubt—the best sons, in every respect, that two parents could ever wish for. You continue to amaze us with all of your accomplishments. We are always so proud of you. And it goes without saying that you are both incredibly loving nephews to your Uncle Mark. My sincere gratitude for publishing this book and bringing my dream to life.

To Adam Reingold: Nobody can ever fault you for lack of patience! You sure needed it working with me. You deserve a medal! I would like to express my deepest gratitude to you, my editor and mentor—and now my third son—for your unwavering support throughout this journey. Without your guidance and leadership, I would have never been able to fulfill my lifetime wish. You're the best!

To Anni Matsick: The moment I spotted your artistic talent, I knew you were the one I wanted to illustrate my book. Your artwork brought the words to life and captured the emotions that were so important to this story. Thank you for all of your efforts and cooperation. You have created a true "work of art."

To Kristine Bergenheim: Your layout of each page and book design are beautifully done. All of your input, time, creativity, and efforts are so much appreciated. What a pleasure it was to work with you.

My sincere gratitude ***to all of you*** who gave me your professional feedback and suggestions as we revised manuscript after manuscript. You know who you are! Thank you so much.

And last but not least, to our precious family dog, ***Sparkie***. Good Boy! Your endless energy, devotion, antics, and unconditional love brought us such happiness. Thank you for being such an important part of our family.

About Braille

Imagine a life in which you could not read or write or share information and ideas with others. Mark's life changed once he was able to learn Braille. Braille enables a blind person to read and write, just like the printed word does for a sighted person.

In 1812, a three-year-old boy in France named Louis Braille injured one of his eyes with a sharp tool while playing in his Dad's saddle shop. Soon both eyes became infected. By the time he was five years old, he was totally blind.

When Louis started school, he could only learn by listening. He was determined to find a way for the blind to read and write. At age 15, he invented a new system called Braille which uses raised dots on a page that could be read by touch. Soon people around the world were using Braille to read and write. Today, thanks to Louis Braille's invention, people like Mark can enrich their lives by being able to read and write.

Braille Activities

Read and review the contents of the Braille card on the **back inside cover**. Then collaborate with your classmates to answer the following questions:

1 Read the last four Braille lines on the card by using the alphabet chart. What do the lines say?

2 What do the three Braille symbols that are not letters or numbers on the card stand for?

3 How does a Braille user know the difference between letters and numbers?

4 What letters are also used as numbers?